ELEGANCE IN ENGINEERING
THE CLASSIC BRITISH STEAM LOCOMOTIVE

W0007935

Colin Alexander & Alon Siton

AMBERLEY

First published 2020

Amberley Publishing
The Hill, Stroud
Gloucestershire, GL5 4EP

www.amberley-books.com

Copyright © Colin Alexander & Alon Siton, 2020

The right of Colin Alexander & Alon Siton to
be identified as the Authors of this work has
been asserted in accordance with the Copyrights,
Designs and Patents Act 1988.

ISBN 978 1 4456 8621 9 (print)
ISBN 978 1 4456 8622 6 (ebook)

British Library Cataloguing in Publication Data.
A catalogue record for this book is available from
the British Library.

Origination by Amberley Publishing.
Printed in the UK.

Introduction

In the words of A. J. Lewer in his 1956 hand-illustrated *The Appreciation of British Steam Locomotive Design*, 'A well-designed engine must be beautiful and efficient.' B. R. Davies added, 'The derivation of modern engine design is an illustration of how a design convention is slowly built up by practical experiment, and shows the close interrelationship between mechanical problems and problems of line and form. The story of the railway engine is in fact a demonstration of the underlying necessity of good design.'

The content of this book was always going to be subjective, for my opinion of what constitutes aesthetic elegance in engineering will differ from that of many people. Beauty is, after all, in the eye of the beholder. The simple premise of this book is that, to my mind's eye, the majority of British steam locomotives, particularly of the late nineteenth and early twentieth centuries, successfully combined the latest engineering innovation with graceful proportions and a clean, uncluttered outline. In short, they were beautiful pieces of machinery. The same cannot always be said for contemporary overseas locomotives, which often seemed to lack that touch of elegance, their engineers perhaps being more concerned with mechanical efficiency or ease of maintenance. I am not for one moment suggesting that there were no ugly British locomotives whatsoever, or that no objects of mechanical beauty ever turned a shapely wheel in other countries.

Chicago architect Louis Sullivan (1856–1924) coined the phrase 'form follows function', and he could easily have been referring to any number of British locomotives of his era. The classic Victorian express passenger engine featured large diameter driving wheels concealed beneath gracefully curving splashers. The lovingly polished boiler would be surmounted by an ornate chimney, sculpted dome and safety valve cover. Many companies embellished their machines with brass and copper ornamentation and the whole thing would be lavishly painted in a distinctive, often colourful, livery with intricate lining, numerals and lettering with painted shadows or on cast plates, and ostentatious coats of arms.

As well as the myriad shades of green favoured by so many companies, others chose a more distinctive livery, such as the rich blues of the Caledonian Railway and the Great Eastern, the Midland's famous Crimson Lake or Mr Stroudley's 'improved engine green' on the London, Brighton & South Coast Railway. This colour was, of course, a fairly bright shade of amber.

Moving parts were usually discreetly concealed, which would make maintenance difficult, but these wonders of the machine age were an aesthetic triumph. In contrast, many locomotives built overseas were, to some British eyes, less attractive, with a clutter of visible pipework and auxiliary equipment attached to the exterior.

The practice was not restricted to top-link express locomotives, for the majority of British goods engines, shunting tanks, industrial locomotives and even narrow-gauge engines were also usually of pleasing outline and proportion, and were sometimes equally ornate in decoration.

The earliest locomotives consisted of a primitive boiler mounted directly on the running gear, with no frames to speak of. Robert Stephenson's *Rocket* was perhaps the first locomotive to which any aesthetic attention was given. Her bright colour scheme and flared, fluted chimney were purely for cosmetic purposes – no doubt to make an impact at the Rainhill Trials.

Perhaps reflecting the modesty of Victorian dress, subsequent locomotives began to hide their vulgar reciprocating motion between the frames that were now carrying their boilers. Indeed, following on from the *Rocket*, most locomotives were built with inside cylinders, until the advent of three- and four-cylindered engines necessitated the mounting of cylinders outside the frames.

As locomotive development entered the Victorian era and traffic increased, locomotives became larger and more powerful. This evolution continued until the 1920s when the British loading gauge restricted anything larger. As boilers grew in diameter, chimneys and domes had to reduce in height to fit within those constraints. The aesthetic beauty of the locomotive was not compromised by this growth, though, and it could be argued that some of the most beautiful and imposing machines ever built emerged in the period between the two world wars.

Certain wheel arrangements seemed to lend themselves to aesthetic beauty, such as passenger engines of 2-4-0, 4-4-0, 4-2-2, 4-4-2 (known as Atlantics) and 4-6-2 (Pacific) configuration, almost always resulting in beautiful proportions. Others that usually 'looked right' include the 2-8-0 (Consolidation) freight locomotive and 0-4-4, 2-6-2 (Prairie) and 2-6-4 tank engines.

The Second World War brought new ideas, and a shortage of manpower led to a need for locomotives that were easier to maintain, with increased accessibility to the parts that required regular maintenance. Although this gave many post-war locomotives a more austere appearance, some would argue their very simplicity gave them an elegance all of their own.

Thankfully, much of Britain's engineering elegance is preserved for posterity, with many locomotives in working order, and many restored in their original ornate liveries for all to appreciate. As well as preservation, the book highlights some of the remarkable new-build projects that have recreated full-scale working replicas of locomotive types that were lost to scrap, beginning with Peppercorn A1 No. 60163 *Tornado*. Another such project is the G5 Locomotive Company's scheme to build a new North Eastern Railway Class O 0-4-4T, and I would like to thank Tim Taylor of that organisation.

Thanks also to Alon Siton for his encouragement and photographic collection, similarly to Tony Hisgett, the invaluable RCTS Photographic Archive and the excellent ETH Zurich resource for their cooperation.

Illustrating the earliest days of the locomotive, before aesthetics played any part in its design, this is the wonderful working replica of Buddle and Chapman's 1815 *Steam Elephant*, for use at Wallsend Colliery on the Tyne. These early machines were effectively stationary engines mounted on wheels, with vertical motion on top of the boiler. Every part of her is purely functional, with no embellishments or thought given to her appearance. Like the other replica early locomotives in use on Beamish Museum's Pockerley Wagonway, she is a remarkable machine and fascinating to watch. (Colin Alexander)

The brilliant father and son team of George and Robert Stephenson designed the legendary *Rocket* for the Liverpool & Manchester Railway. She was the first 'single', having one driving axle, and the ungainly vertical motion of her predecessors was replaced by graceful inclined cylinders driving the front wheels directly and smoothly via crank pins. This allowed her to reach the unprecedented speed of 35 mph and gave her a rakish appearance, enhanced by her bright yellow colour scheme. *Rocket* is conserved in a greatly modified form as part of the Science Museum collection. In 2018, she returned 'home' temporarily to Newcastle's Discovery Museum, half a mile from the site where she was built in 1829, and is seen here alongside another nineteenth-century Tyneside engineering icon, Sir Charles Parsons' *Turbinia*. (Colin Alexander)

The Stephensons' works in Newcastle was also responsible for building the first truly successful locomotives for Isambard Kingdom Brunel's 7-foot-¼-inch-gauge Great Western Railway. Among them was 2-2-2 *North Star* of 1837. This wheel arrangement was a natural progression from the Stephensons' 0-2-2 and 2-2-0 designs. While initially saved for preservation, sadly today a full-sized replica in Swindon's Steam Museum has to suffice. There is a pleasing symmetry to her wheel arrangement, set off by the flared chimney and polished brasswork. Notice also that her motion is entirely out of sight, concealed between her frames. (Alon Siton collection)

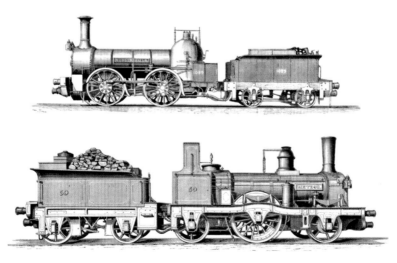

It didn't take long for the pioneering Stockton & Darlington Railway to progress from vertical-motion coal haulers, like George Stephenson's *Locomotion*, to motive power of a more elegant appearance. 2-2-2 No. 50 *Meteor*, with her subtly curved outside frames, was built at the railway's own Shildon works in 1843 for passenger service. 0-4-0 No. 1089 *Huddersfield* was built by Messrs Bury & Co. in 1846 for mineral workings. She features that company's trademark 'haystack' firebox. Illustration from *The Engineer*, 26 December 1879. (Alon Siton collection)

A mere fourteen years have elapsed since *Rocket* took the Rainhill Trials by storm and locomotive development has moved on apace, not least in the size of the boiler. Showing clear evolution from *North Star* seen above, the Great Western Railway's Iron Duke Class of 1843 was an early example of the classic 4-2-2 wheel arrangement. This particular locomotive carries the name *Amazon* on her elegant outside frames. (Alon Siton collection)

Built in 1845 for the Grand Junction Railway, Francis Trevithick's 2-2-2 *Columbine* was photographed for posterity below the medieval walls at York, on the site of the city's original station. She is now preserved in the Science Museum in Kensington, where she is displayed without her outsized cab, which was a later addition. In original condition, she was a little beauty with her outside motion located in elegant slotted frames, and smooth reverse curves uniting her smokebox and cylinders. (Alon Siton collection)

Also to the design of Francis Trevithick, London & North Western Railway 2-2-2 No. 3020 *Cornwall* of 1847 was one of the most unusual locomotives of her time. Her 8-foot diameter driving wheels permitted Trevithick to place her boiler below the driving axle, providing a low centre of gravity. She was rebuilt by Ramsbottom along more conventional lines, in which condition she is seen here. Compare her framing to that of *Columbine* and note how Trevithick has continued the slotted motion, but now horizontally. (ETH Zurich)

Cornwall is now preserved and spent some time at the Buckinghamshire Railway Centre, Quainton Road, where this shot of her spectacular splasher and brass nameplate were taken. She is now at Locomotion, Shildon. (Paul Jones)

Certain classic British passenger 2-2-2 types were known as 'Jenny Linds', after the Swedish opera singer. Many such locomotives were built for export, as in the case of the Barcelona–Mataró railway, who ordered four from Joseph Wright & Sons of Saltley, Birmingham, in 1848. This is a replica, built for its centenary, at the excellent museum in Vilanova i la Geltrú. The replica is not exact, having smaller driving wheels than the original 6-foot 2-inch diameter, but her elegant appearance is British throughout. (Bonaventura Leris)

A double-headed train on Scotland's North British Railway features an outside-framed 2-2-2 and an inside-framed 0-4-2. The 'single' dates from 1849 and is numbered 1009. She is an early exponent of the fluted splasher favoured by many designers of the Victorian era. The image also illustrates a move towards a corporate style, with both locomotives possessing similar cabs and boiler mountings. (Alon Siton collection)

Right and below: Yet another London & North Western Railway 2-2-2 type was the Bloomer Class, designed by J. Edward McConnell in 1851. He was locomotive superintendent of that company's southern division, while Trevithick was in charge further north. None of these handsome locomotives survived, but a non-working full-scale replica was built at Wolverton in 1991, and she was displayed on a plinth in Milton Keynes for many years. Her inside-cylinder layout and simplified splasher design are in contrast to Trevithick practice, but the tall, elegant chimney is a typical Victorian design feature. (Photographs by Lewis Bevan and Michael Brace)

One of the most spectacular locomotive types ever to run in Britain was James Pearson's astonishing 4-2-4 tank of 1853, of which fourteen examples were built for the broad-gauge Bristol & Exeter Railway. Eight of them had flangeless driving wheels 9 feet in diameter, which, together with the tall chimney permitted by that railway's generous loading gauge, made for a very imposing appearance. (Tony Hisgett collection)

With the intricate curved cut-outs in her splashers and the delicate lining applied to her sturdy outside frames, aesthetics was clearly a consideration of this experimental 4-2-2, built in 1853 by Hawthorn's in Newcastle for the Great Northern Railway. No. 215 was a standard-gauge version of Gooch's GWR broad-gauge 4-2-2s, but her rigid leading wheel arrangement led to a derailment soon after entering service. (Alon Siton collection)

This pretty little 0-4-0WT is the only surviving standard-gauge locomotive built by George England. No. 5 is part of the National Collection and was built in 1857 for Captain William Peel of the Sandy & Potton Railway. In 1862 she was sold to the L&NWR and was employed at Crewe works, where she was given the name *Shannon*. By 1878 she was working for the Wantage Tramway, and eventually passed to the GWR. Happily, she is preserved at Didcot, as seen here. (Ian J. Robinson)

No. 87 was one of Benjamin Conner's 2-2-2s for the Caledonian Railway, built from 1859 onwards, with enormous 8-foot-2-inch-diameter driving wheels for express passenger service. This image shows her as rebuilt by Drummond with a new boiler and cab, but retaining the distinctive radially fluted splashers. Like *Cornwall*, seen earlier, the slide bars for her reciprocating outside motion are incorporated into the frames. (Tony Hisgett collection)

This neat 2-4-0 is North British Railway Class E115 No. 392. Twenty-four of these locomotives were built in Glasgow by Dübs and Neilson between 1861 and 1867. Her crew have clearly taken pride in their steed, judging by her condition, but the Westinghouse pump on her running plate detracts slightly from her otherwise uncluttered appearance. (Alon Siton collection)

The North London Railway possessed some distinctive 4-4-0T engines, initially of inside-cylinder configuration and with cutaway water tanks allowing access to the leading driving wheels. Note the unusual outside-framed front bogie. In contrast to NBR No. 392 (seen above), the crew of NLR No. 107 do not appear to have cleaned their machine in a while, but no amount of grime can conceal her good looks. (ETH Zurich)

The oldest working standard-gauge steam engine in Britain is Furness Railway 0-4-0 No. 20, owned by the Furness Railway Trust. She was built in 1863 by Sharp Stewart of Manchester and later rebuilt as a saddle tank. This remarkable preservation survivor shows off her beautifully simple Victorian outline in this delightful broadside study, coupled to a vintage Midland Railway brake van at Swanwick on 8 May 2001. (Ian Duffield)

Joseph Beattie's 0298 Class 2-4-0WT was designed for suburban traffic on the busy London & South Western Railway, and the first of the eighty-five-strong class was introduced in 1863. Remarkably, three locomotives survived into British Railways' ownership and two are preserved, which is fortunate for aficionados of Victorian steam. Nos 30585 and 30587 are seen together, their curves muted slightly by their plain post-nationalisation livery, at the Buckinghamshire Railway Centre, Quainton Road. (Peter Stott)

In contrast to some of the high-stepping 'singles' seen previously, the driving wheels of London Brighton & South Coast Railway 2-2-2 No. 490 *Dieppe* appear positively tiny. Of very pleasing proportions nonetheless, she was built by Robert Stephenson & Co. in 1864 to the design of John Craven. This image, thought to depict her on the turntable at Singleton, Sussex, shows her in an unusually dirty condition for a Victorian locomotive. (Tony Hisgett collection)

There is no disguising the British lineage of this Beyer Peacock 2-4-0, No. 56 of the Staatsspoorwegen (State Railways Company of the Netherlands). She was built in Manchester in 1866 and lasted in service until 1929. The brass edging of her splashers, incorporating the builder's name, was a trademark of many Beyer Peacock exports. Her boiler mountings are equally elegant. (Alon Siton collection)

The beautiful crimson lake livery and lining of the Midland Railway is shown to great effect on the sturdy outside frames of the only surviving Kirtley 2-4-0. No. 158A is displayed inside the Swanwick Exhibition Hall at the Midland Railway Centre, Derbyshire. Twenty-nine of them were built from 1866, and No. 158A enjoyed a career lasting eighty-one years. She is now part of the National Collection. (Colin Alexander)

The Stephenson 'long-boiler' 0-6-0 type had a short wheelbase for negotiating sharp curves, which allowed for a deep firebox behind the rear axle. No. E18 was built in Newcastle in 1866 for the New South Wales Government Railway in Australia. Her tidy, unmistakeably British outline can be admired today in the NSW Rail Museum at Thirlmere, near Sydney. (Kevin Bradney)

The mundane Victorian goods locomotive was often adorned with elaborate boiler mountings. Look at the beautifully fluted, almost architectural, dome and safety valve cover on this London Brighton & South Coast Railway 0-6-0. She was another Craven design, built by Manning Wardle in 1866. In contrast to E18, seen above, she has the more conventional equally spaced driving wheels with the firebox between the second and third axles. (Tony Hisgett collection)

Even the humble industrial tank engine of the nineteenth century was usually a splendidly ornate piece of machinery. The Waterloo Main Colliery of Leeds took delivery of this fine 0-6-0ST from the nearby Hunslet Locomotive Works in 1867. She has been given a fully lined-out livery and a magnificent flared chimney, although she lacks protection for her crew. (Alon Siton collection)

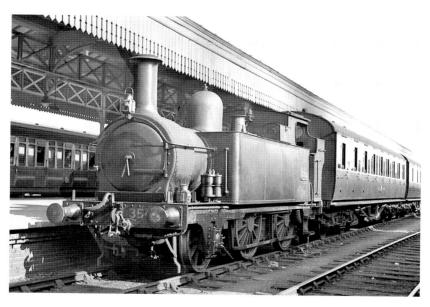

Another long-lived type was Armstrong's Class 455 2-4-0T for the GWR, also known as the 'Metropolitan' or 'Metro' tank. No. 3562 is seen here at Oxford General on 29 July 1948. Like the L&SWR Beattie well tanks of the same wheel arrangement, they were intended for London suburban services, but they were also used on the underground section of the Metropolitan Railway – hence the nickname. So highly regarded were they that 140 of these useful and handsomely simple engines were built from 1868 to 1899. (Reproduced by kind permission of the RCTS Archive)

The Ffestiniog Railway in North Wales pioneered the use of the Double Fairlie 0-4-4-0T locomotive, a radical design patented in the 1860s. Articulated and with all wheels powered, they were ideal for the steep gradients and tight curves of the 2-foot-gauge, slate-carrying railway from Blaenau Ffestiniog to Porthmadog. *Merddin Emrys*, preserved in working order, dates from 1879 and shows her neat symmetry in the Welsh rain at Porthmadog, 29 May 2019. (Colin Alexander)

The freight version of Kirtley's Midland 2-4-0 (see No. 158A earlier) was the visually similar Class 700 0-6-0, a true Victorian workhorse, of which over 300 were built from 1869 – the last one surviving in service into 1951. Some saw wartime use with the Railway Operating Department (ROD), as seen here. Built by Dübs & Co. in Glasgow, No. 2717 was sent to France and became isolated in no man's land at Cambrai in 1917. After capture by the German army, she was used on their military railway near Brussels then repatriated after the war. Her extended cab roof, presumably to give her crew some wartime protection, does not detract from her rugged good looks. (Alon Siton collection)

Another British locomotive for the Empire, this time the Scinde, Punjab & Delhi Railway. Built at Robert Stephenson's in 1869, this is 0-4-2 No. 47 *Eagle*. Other than the presence of the scallop-edged sunshade over her footplate, she would not look out of place on any pre-grouping line in Britain. She is now preserved in Moghalpura works at Lahore, in present-day Pakistan. (Alon Siton collection)

One of the most iconic Victorian locomotives is Patrick Stirling's 'single' for express passenger services on the Great Northern Railway. 4-2-2 No. 1 of 1870 is seen here at her Doncaster birthplace on the occasion of the works' 150th anniversary in 2003. She is part of the National Collection and embodies everything that is elegant about British engineering of the period, with her symphony of curves and graceful 8-foot-diameter driving wheels. (Colin Alexander)

At the other end of the scale from Stirling's East Coast thoroughbred is the London Brighton & South Coast Railway's A1 Terrier Class 0-6-0T, introduced by Stroudley in 1872. Several of these pretty little tank engines are preserved, including the iconic No. 55 *Stepney*, seen here at Sheffield Park on the Bluebell Railway. She gained fame as the eponymous star of Revd W. Awdry's *Stepney the "Bluebell" Engine*, alongside the legendary Thomas. Her livery is Stroudley's 'Improved Engine Green'. (Colin Alexander)

Just as the Double Fairlie is synonymous with the Ffestiniog Railway, the Isle of Man Steam Railway is associated with these wonderful Beyer Peacock 2-4-0Ts, introduced in 1873. No. 9 *Fenella* and No. 13 *Kissack* await their next turns at Douglas on 8 May 2016. Notice the Beyer Peacock trademark running plate sloping gracefully over the inclined cylinders. (Kenny Alexander)

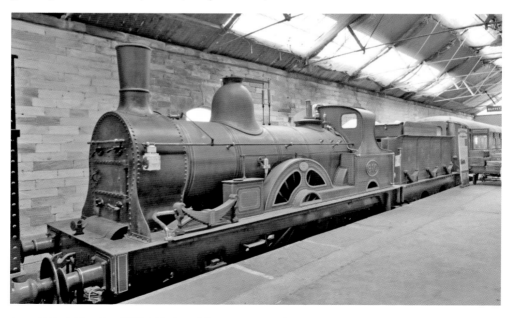

As a child, visiting the old York Railway Museum with my father was always a treat, for, without exception, every locomotive in there was a work of engineering artistry. Much of its collection is now in the 'new' museum, but 1875-built North Eastern Railway Fletcher 901 Class 2-4-0 No. 910 is on loan at the Stainmore Railway, where her ornate brasswork is displayed inside Kirkby Stephen East station. (Ian R. Simpson)

Possibly even more famous than *Stepney*, certainly to people of a certain generation, is the *Green Dragon*, star of *The Railway Children*. In fact, she was 1876-built Lancashire & Yorkshire Railway 'Ironclad' 0-6-0 No. 957, designed by Barton Wright, and she appeared alongside Jenny Agutter and Bernard Cribbins in the classic film. Seen here at Haworth shed, Keighley & Worth Valley Railway, on 2 March 2013 in a more authentic livery than the one she wore on the silver screen, she shows how even a simple lined black colour scheme can be very attractive. (Bill Pugsley)

Here is another Welsh narrow-gauge locomotive sharing a neatness of appearance with her larger counterparts. Built in 1878 at Hughes' Locomotive & Tramway Engine Works, Loughborough, this is former Corris Railway 0-4-0ST, later converted to an 0-4-2ST to cope with the sharp curves on the line. When that railway closed she became *Sir Haydn* on the Talyllyn Railway, where she remains. The revived Corris Railway has plans to recreate a new-build replacement. (Colin Alexander)

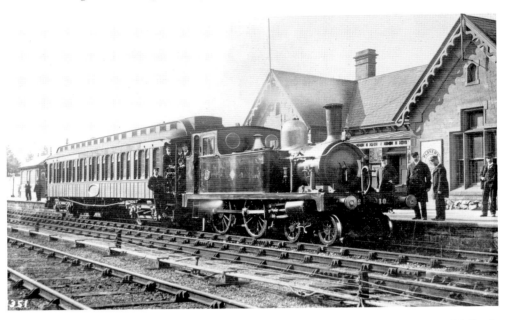

The Midland & Great Northern Joint Railway was a relatively small concern connecting the Midlands to the Lincolnshire fens and the Norfolk Broads. Locomotive No. 10 was an elegant Hudswell Clarke outside-cylindered 4-4-0T with a very capacious side-windowed cab, built originally for the Lynn & Fakenham Railway. She is seen here coupled to an equally elegant former Midland Railway Pullman car at Wirksworth station. (Alon Siton collection)

Once again proving that freight locomotives can be just as good-looking as their more glamorous passenger stablemates, is the L&NWR 'Coal Tank' 0-6-2T, of which 300 were built from 1881. Preservation survivor No. 1054 conveys an appearance of functional, handsome simplicity at Keighley on 21 June 2014. (Richard Fox)

Staying with the tank locomotive theme, Adams' graceful 0415 Class 4-4-2 Radial Tank was an 1882 design for the L&SWR. As in the case of the Beattie well tanks, long after the majority were scrapped, three survived into BR ownership, until 1961, for operating the Lyme Regis branch. Neilson-built No. 488 is preserved at the Bluebell Railway, as seen here at Sheffield Park. (Colin Alexander)

The LB&SCR was not unique, but was certainly unusual in its use of the 0-4-2 wheel arrangement for express passenger trains. Stroudley's locomotives were always handsome affairs, and No. 175 *Hayling* is no exception. Note how the cab side sheets and splashers make a smooth, radiused transition with the running board. No. 214 *Gladstone* is preserved in the National Railway Museum, York. (Tony Hisgett)

Later to find greater fame with the North Eastern Railway, T. W. Worsdell established his reputation by designing some very attractive and effective locomotives for the Great Eastern. One of his greatest successes at Stratford was his 1883 Class Y14 (L&NER J15) 0-6-0. They would form the basis for his later NER C Class. A total of 289 Y14s were built by 1913 and one is preserved – No. 65462, seen here in action at Weybourne on the North Norfolk Railway. (Charles Woodland)

Another eye-pleasing 0-6-0 was the GWR's 2301 Class, which became known simply as the 'Dean Goods'. These robust engines were introduced in 1883 and many saw wartime service overseas with the Railway Operating Department. No. 2516 is preserved at Swindon, looking splendid in GWR green with polished brass and copper, but this is its long-lost sister No. 2411, looking rather unkempt in British Railways days. (Alon Siton collection)

One of the more famous types to emerge from Beyer Peacock's Gorton Foundry was the distinctive condensing 4-4-0T for the first underground line in the world – London's Metropolitan Railway. They worked that intensive service until electrification in 1905. No. 63 was built in 1884 and is an excellent example of a bespoke design to a narrow specification, which is nevertheless an aesthetic success. Sister engine No. 23 can still be seen in the London Transport Museum at Covent Garden. (Alon Siton collection)

Following his Radial Tanks, the L&SWR's William Adams introduced his Class 460 express passenger 4-4-0 tender locomotive. They were among the first British outside-cylindered machines of that classic wheel arrangement, built for speed with elegant large-diameter driving wheels. Introduced in 1884, twenty-one were built by Neilson and by Robert Stephenson & Co., including one built by the latter firm specifically for the 1887 Jubilee exhibition in Newcastle. (ETH Zurich)

Clearly continuing the lineage from No. 910, seen earlier, North Eastern Railway 2-4-0 No. 1463 was designed by a committee headed by Henry Tennant. The locomotive was essentially a simplified version of the successful 901 Class, featuring cleaner lines and less ornamentation than her predecessor. She is exhibited inside Darlington's North Road Museum, as seen on 24 October 2015. (Colin Alexander)

I always admired the looks of the Midland Class 3F 0-6-0, compared to the top-heavy appearance of the more powerful 4F derivative. They were introduced by Johnson on the Midland Railway in 1885 and developed by Fowler. The great longevity of the class is exemplified by BR No. 43645, easing off the turntable at Evesham's Midland shed in 1962. (Anthony Haynes)

The New South Wales Government Office of Heritage and Environment describe X10 Class 2-4-0T No. 1033, which is in their care, as 'an attractive small engine produced in England in the late 19th century with a polished brass dome (painted black at the time of this photograph), tall chimney and large wheels'. She was built by Beyer Peacock in 1885 and is preserved at Thirlmere. (Kevin Bradney)

If the adjective 'cheeky' could ever be applied to a locomotive, this is it. The Lancashire & Yorkshire Railway Class 21 0-4-0ST, nicknamed the 'Pug', was a childhood OO-gauge favourite, constructed from a Kitmaster plastic kit. Of sixty built from 1886, two are preserved, including No. 51218, seen here at Newton Heath, celebrating her centenary in 2001. Note her 'dumb' buffers, a feature more commonly associated with industrial locomotives. (Andrew Brindley)

By 1886, T. W. Worsdell had parted company with the Great Eastern and had been appointed locomotive engineer to the North Eastern Railway. He built upon his success with the Y14/J15 (seen above) with the introduction of his C Class 0-6-0, later L&NER J21 – very much the typical, unfussy late Victorian goods engine in appearance. A total of 201 were built. NER No. 876 was still in service until 1962 as BR No. 65033. Since then she has entered preservation and is seen here at Doncaster. (Colin Alexander)

Widely regarded as one of the most attractive of Victorian locomotives was Drummond's celebrated 'single', a one-off for the Caledonian Railway. 4-2-2 No. 123 was built by Neilson of Glasgow in 1886 and participated in the legendary Race to the North. She was also employed as a Royal Train pilot. Withdrawn and preserved by the LM&SR in 1935, she was restored to working order in 1958 and hauled a number of enthusiasts' specials. She is seen here at Callander East around 1964. She now resides in Glasgow's excellent Riverside Museum. (Alon Siton collection)

No. 1757 was one of Johnson's beautiful 4-4-0s for the Midland Railway, with 7-foot ½-inch driving wheels and built in 1886. She was unusual for that company in carrying a name. *Beatrice* was exhibited at the Royal Jubilee Saltaire Exhibition of 1887, where she won a gold medal. She was named after Princess Beatrice, who opened the exhibition. She was also given the honour of hauling the Royal Train, taking Queen Victoria from Derby to Scotland in May 1891. (Tony Hisgett collection)

The workaday 0-6-0T should not be overlooked in the beauty stakes. James Holden, having succeeded T. W. Worsdell at Stratford, designed the T18 Class for the GER. It was so effective that all subsequent 0-6-0 tanks for that company derived from it. Fifty were built from 1886 and the last one was withdrawn in 1962, having become Class J66 under the L&NER. (Tony Hisgett collection)

L&NWR No. 955 *Charles Dickens* was an example of F. W. Webb's Improved Precedent Class 2-4-0 for express passenger work on the West Coast Main Line. A total of 168 were built at Crewe between 1887 and 1901, and one, No. 790 *Hardwicke*, is preserved as part of the National Collection. Her fame arose from her 1895 exploits during the Race to the North against the rival East Coast companies. She took just two hours six minutes to cover 141 miles from Crewe to Carlisle over Shap Summit, averaging 67.1 mph and, in doing so, setting a speed record. A perfect combination of grace and pace. (Tony Hisgett collection)

The classic lines of an archetypal British inside-cylinder 4-4-0 passenger engine are enhanced by the photographic grey livery for this official workshop portrait of No. 700. She was one of thirty-one that were built from 1887 to the design of Thomas Parker for the Manchester, Sheffield & Lincolnshire Railway (later to become the Great Central Railway), Classes 2 and 2A. Becoming L&NER Class D7, all were scrapped but a project is underway for a new-build replica. (Alon Siton collection)

So successful was Aspinall's Class 27 0-6-0 for the Lancashire & Yorkshire Railway that nearly 500 were built between 1889 and 1918 – yet another typical British goods engine of rugged, modest outline. Sole survivor, former L&YR No. 1300, later BR No. 52322, is seen here inside the shed at Buckley Wells, Bury, on the East Lancashire Railway in July 2019. (Colin Alexander)

Also on the L&YR in 1889, and almost as numerous, were the extremely handsome 1008 Class 2-4-2T engines. A total of 310 were built and they did sterling service on passenger trains for decades. Doyen of the class, No. 1008, is seen here as preserved in the 1980s, at Tyseley. She is now on display in the National Railway Museum in York. (Reproduced by kind permission of the RCTS Archive)

The 0-4-4T wheel arrangement, as mentioned in the introduction, was one of those configurations that invariably seemed to produce locomotives that were pleasing to the eye. Adams built sixty Class O2 engines for the L&SWR from 1889. Many were transferred to the Isle of Wight, where No. W24 *Calbourne* survives in preservation. Here she is paying a visit to the mainland at Ropley on the Mid-Hants Railway. (Colin D. Lee)

If you were to conduct a poll among British steam enthusiasts asking their opinion on the most handsome locomotive, Johnson's Midland Railway 4-2-2s, such as No. 1865, would be near the top of the charts. Ninety-five of them were built at Derby in 1889–90, and thankfully one, No. 673, can be seen in all her Crimson Lake glory in the National Collection at York. They were known as 'Spinners' because their reciprocating parts were discreetly hidden, giving an almost effortless appearance when in motion. (Tony Hisgett collection)

Some more handsome exports, this time in Portugal, where 1890-built Beyer Peacock cousins 0-6-2T No. CP014 and long-boiler 0-6-0 No. CP23 are seen together at Viana do Castelo in 1990. While the outsized headlamps are pure Portuguese practice, their brass domes and copper chimney caps, as well as their general neatness, betray their British origins. (Nigel Menzies)

Compared to his 460 Class seen earlier, Adams' X2 4-4-0 for the L&SWR had larger driving wheels, bigger cylinders and higher boiler pressure. They were also an aesthetic improvement; the previous rectangular cab sides were replaced by the curves seen here. Twenty were built at Nine Elms from 1890, of which No. 577, photographed at Wimbledon, was the first. (Tony Hisgett collection)

Another Beyer Peacock design for New South Wales was the Z20 Class 2-6-4T, introduced in 1890. The preserved example here at Thirlmere, No. 2029, was part of a later series built locally at the railway's own Eveleigh workshops. They were versatile, being equally at home hauling coal or passengers. Although her inside-cylindered configuration is somewhat archaic for such a large tank locomotive, she possesses a dignified, purposeful appearance. (Kevin Bradney)

Sir Nigel Gresley said, 'When the 2-2-2-2 type *Greater Britain* was built it was thought that the limit in size and power of the locomotive had been almost reached, and when, in an excess of loyal zeal she was painted crimson, and another engine of the same class, *Queen Empress*, was painted white at the time of the Queen's Diamond Jubilee, surely the limits of artistic resource of the locomotive engineer were attained.' Webb's compound 'double singles', introduced in 1891, had their front 'drivers' powered by the inside cylinder, with the outside cylinders driving the rear set. (Alon Siton collection)

While the L&NWR was pushing the boundaries of possibility, the GWR Dean's outside-framed 2-2-2s, such as No. 3013, could not have been more conventional in their compact symmetry. Unfortunately, looks aren't everything and a problem with weight distribution led to unsteadiness and a serious derailment. As a result, the entire class of eighty locomotives was rebuilt with a leading bogie, as 4-2-2s. (ETH Zurich)

This pretty 2-4-0, No. 420, is one of James Holden's Class T26 mixed-traffic locomotives for the Great Eastern Railway, introduced in 1891. The 100 members of the class proved extremely useful and versatile, even finding work in L&NER days on the treacherous Stainmore route of the former North Eastern Railway. The last survivor was withdrawn from British Railways in 1959 as No. 62785, and is preserved in the National Collection in original blue livery as No. 490, in which condition she is displayed at Bressingham in Norfolk. (Tony Hisgett)

During the European colonial era, it was not only the railways of the British Empire that ordered locomotives from British companies. Nederlandsch-Indische Spoorweg Maatschappij (the Dutch East Indies Railway) operated the standard-gauge system in what is now Java. Beyer Peacock 0-4-2 No. 28 was built at the Gorton Foundry in 1893 to an entirely British aesthetic. Note the brass builders' plate incorporated into the splasher. (Alon Siton collection)

Apart from the unusually large cut-outs on her cab sides, this Neilson-built 4-4-0 for the East Indian Railway would look very much at home in Edwardian Scotland. No. 213 was built in 1913 and displays classic British motifs such as full lining, sandbox combined with splasher, flared chimney and tender sides, a round dome and smokebox wing plates. (Alon Siton collection)

Perfectly balanced in the visual sense, with her outside-framed carrying wheels, is James Holden's Great Eastern Railway Class C32 2-4-2T of 1893. No. 1085 was one of fifty built, later becoming L&NER Class F3. Some carried condensing gear, hence the long pipe above the water tank, and the last one was withdrawn in the 1950s. (Tony Hisgett)

T. W. Worsdell was replaced by his brother, Wilson, on the North Eastern Railway in 1890, and one of his most enduring designs was the Class O 0-4-4T – in my opinion the prettiest of tank locomotive designs. A total of 110 were built, later becoming L&NER Class G5, and they served until ousted by diesels in the late 1950s. Looking extremely smart in her lined BR black livery, at Pateley Bridge, in 1951, is No. 67253. Unfortunately, none survived, but the Class G5 Locomotive Company is building the 111th example at Shildon, County Durham. I look forward to seeing her in steam in the not-too-distant future. (Geoff Horsman, courtesy of the Armstrong Trust)

Dübs & Co. of Glasgow works No. 3405 of 1896 was this outside-cylindered 4-4-0 for the Highland Railway, No. 132 *Loch Naver*. She was one of eighteen such locomotives designed by David Jones, who found fame when he introduced Britain's first 4-6-0. His locomotives' cabs were much more rectangular than those to which Victorian eyes were accustomed, but that does not detract from the tidy appearance of No. 132. (Alon Siton collection)

Sir Alec Issigonis, designer of the Morris Minor and the legendary Mini, is credited with describing the camel as a 'horse designed by a committee'. This could well be the locomotive equivalent! This magnificent specimen of the European Continental aesthetic was built in 1896 by Krauss for the Royal Bavarian State Railway. No. 1400 is best described as a 4-2-2-2, on which the extra booster wheels in front of the larger drivers could be raised and lowered as necessary. (Tony Hisgett collection)

The popular imagination was captured in the late Victorian era by a notorious series of speed exploits in a publicity exercise that became known as the Race to the North. This involved the rival companies on the West and East Coast routes incrementally shaving time from their schedules from London to Aberdeen. In its quest for speed, the NER's Wilson Worsdell built a pair of locomotives with the largest diameter coupled wheels of any British locomotive – at 7 feet 1¼ inches – the Class Q1 4-4-0s. They featured neat combined splashers incorporated into the sides of the clerestory-roofed cab. No. 1870 is seen here at York. (Tony Hisgett collection)

The Great Western, meanwhile, persisted with outside frames for its 4-4-0s, and Dean introduced his Badminton Class in 1897, developed from the Dukes. No. 3293 *Barrington* was photographed as rebuilt with a taper boiler, alongside a typical GWR coaling stage. Her curved running plate is particularly pleasing to the eye, and the distinctive brass safety valve cover would be a Swindon trademark until nationalisation. (ETH Zurich)

As locomotives were absorbed by larger companies, they did not always suit their new colour schemes. Former London, Brighton & South Coast Railway Class E4 0-6-2T No. 473 (formerly named *Birch Grove*) designed in 1897 by Robert Billinton looks quite at home in her Southern Railway lined green livery. The photograph was taken at Sheffield Park on the Bluebell Railway in 2012. (Colin Alexander)

By 1898, Drummond had replaced Jones as locomotive superintendent of the Highland Railway, and his well-proportioned inside-cylindered 4-4-0s now reigned supreme. LM&SR No. 14398 *Ben Alder* was one of twenty 'Small Bens' and was originally HR No. 2. She was withdrawn in 1953 and was set aside for preservation. She lasted until 1967 when she was sadly scrapped, possibly because her original boiler had been replaced by one of Caledonian Railway origin. (Alon Siton collection)

Locomotives continued to increase in size and power, but aesthetic considerations were not compromised. Built in 1898, No. 990 *Henry Oakley* had the distinction of being the only named locomotive on the Great Northern Railway until Gresley's first Pacifics of 1922. She was Britain's first 4-4-2, designed by Henry Ivatt, and is now part of the National Collection. She is seen displayed at an open day at her Doncaster birthplace in 2003. (Colin Alexander)

Contrast Ivatt's dignified GNR Atlantic above with the vulgarity of an Austrian contemporary, built by Karl Gölsdorf in 1898. There is not one part of her that is more attractive when compared to the same part of No. 990. No. 901 was an unusual inside-cylinder, outside-framed 4-6-0 with a large steam-collecting drum above the boiler, serving the same purpose as the British dome. (Alon Siton collection)

Despite the grime encrusting her pseudo-North Eastern livery, ex-NER Class E1 0-6-0T, later L&NER Class J72 No. 68723, displays all the attributes of a neat Victorian tank locomotive. They were introduced in 1898 by Wilson Worsdell, and further batches were added up to the 1950s. This photograph was taken at Newcastle Central station in 1963. (Billy Embleton)

Also dating from 1898 and, although designed for humbler duties, still looking every inch the stablemate of *Henry Oakley*, is one of Ivatt's Class C12 4-4-2T engines. Her clean lines cannot be disguised by her filthy paintwork. The photograph was taken beside Stamford signal box in the late 1940s during the post-war period, a time when it was not unusual to see locomotives in a deplorable external condition. (Reproduced by kind permission of the RCTS Archive)

Yet another beautiful inside-cylinder 4-4-0, built in 1898 by Neilson & Co. for the South Eastern Railway to the design of James Stirling, is this Class B. The following year the line would merge with the London, Chatham & Dover to become the South Eastern & Chatham, in whose fine livery No. 447 is portrayed. (Alon Siton collection)

As the nineteenth century drew to a close, passenger traffic on the East Coast Main Line had become so heavy that double-heading was often necessary to cope with demand. Wilson Worsdell's answer was his Class R 4-4-0 for the North Eastern Railway. Not only were they very aesthetically pleasing, they were successful and reliable, with a total of sixty being built at Gateshead. No. 2011, first of the class, was rostered to work from Newcastle to Edinburgh and Leeds almost continuously for two years and the D20s, as they became in L&NER days, managed very high mileages between overhauls. No. 2015, seen here in an official works photograph, ended her days as BR No. 62344 and the last of the class was withdrawn in November 1957. Sadly none survived into preservation. (ETH Zurich)

Also introduced in 1899, another very successful and long-lasting 4-4-0 class was the London & South Western Railway's T9, designed by Drummond and given the nickname 'Greyhounds' for their free-running capabilities. No. 30732 shows off her powerful outline in BR black livery. The last of the sixty-six locomotives to be withdrawn was No. 30120 in 1963, and she is now preserved. Note the unusual eight-wheeled tender with inside bearings. (ETH Zurich)

The valleys of south Wales were home to several independent railway companies before the 1923 grouping, and most of them relied heavily on sturdy 0-6-2Ts, some of which were quite plain in appearance. The Taff Vale Railway was one of those lines, and Neilson-built Class O2 No. 31 of 1899 has some stylish touches, such as the shapely radii on her bunker and delicate lining throughout. (Alon Siton collection)

Some might argue that Robert Billinton's designs for the London, Brighton & South Coast Railway lacked some of the visual panache of his illustrious predecessor, Stroudley. His adoption of Stroudley's 'Improved Engine Green' livery ensured continuity while introducing some modern features such as the raised running plate, seen here on his Class B4 4-4-0, No. 50 *Tasmania*. Thirty-three of them were built from 1899. (Alon Siton collection)

To many people, Holden's Claud Hamilton 4-4-0 locomotives for the Great Eastern Railway, introduced in 1900, were the most handsome engines of all. There were some variations and several rebuilds, but No. 1855 (seen here) is of the D56 type – later L&NER D15, with a Belpaire firebox. She lasted in service as BR No. 62546 until 1957. (Alon Siton collection)

Another classic 0-4-4T in the shape of Caledonian Railway No. 419, the sole survivor of a type introduced in 1900. She is showing off some typical St Rollox touches, such as the decorative copper star on her smokebox door and the beautiful lined Prussian blue and crimson livery. The photograph was taken on 21 October 2007 on the Bo'ness & Kinneil Railway, home of the Scottish Railway Preservation Society. (Ian J. Robinson)

The British goods 0-6-0 changed little over the years, other than the gradual increase in size. One of the prettiest was the SE&CR C Class 0-6-0, introduced by Harry Wainwright in 1900. Preserved No. 592 looks resplendent in her rich, lined green livery and polished brass at Sheffield Park on the Bluebell Railway. (Colin Alexander)

At the dawn of the twentieth century, as the Victorian era came to a close, almost uniquely the 1901 GWR persisted with outside frames, as seen on City Class 4-4-0 No. 3433 *City of Bath*. She is posed in photographic grey livery for her official works portrait. (ETH Zurich)

No. 3433's famous sister, No. 3440 *City of Truro*, is claimed to be the first locomotive to attain the magical 100 mph. Much doubt and controversy has raged in the ensuing years as to the accuracy of the timings of this downhill run with a lightweight mail train. What is certain is that these little engines were capable of high speeds. No. 3440 is preserved and her nameplate is typical of the brass embellishments of the era. (Colin Alexander)

No. 43.

THE VULCAN LOCOMOTIVE WORKS.

SUPERHEATED PASSENGER ENGINE AND TENDER
(3 CYLINDER COMPOUND)
FOR THE
LONDON MIDLAND AND SCOTTISH RAILWAY.

WHEELS 4-4-0 & 6.	GENERAL DIMENSIONS.		GAUGE. 4ft. 8½in.

The year 1902 saw the introduction on the Midland Railway of one of Britain's best looking and most iconic 4-4-0 designs. When the London, Midland & Scottish Railway absorbed the MR in 1923 it perpetuated that company's 'small engine' policy, so while the L&NER built Pacifics and the GWR its large 4-6-0s, the LM&SR continued building Midland Compounds until 1932, reaching a total of 240 locomotives. No. 1184 was one of a batch of twenty-five built by Vulcan Foundry in 1925. (Alon Siton collection)

During the Edwardian period, the size of locomotives increased dramatically, as heavier trains and faster timings become the norm. As we have seen, the GWR continued building outside-framed 4-4-0s of a type firmly rooted in the Victorian era, but paradoxically that company also looked to the future with Churchward's Saint Class 4-6-0, a type that would evolve over the next forty years. All were scrapped but new-build replica No. 2999 *Lady of Legend* can be admired at the Great Western Society headquarters at Didcot. (Alan Burkwood)

The vital heavy freight side of railway operation also needed larger and more powerful locomotives, but this did not result in any aesthetic compromise. Comparison between 1903-built GWR 2-8-0 No. 2807 (seen here at Pickering in September 2016) and No. 2999 (depicted above) demonstrates clearly that goods engines could be just as handsome, as well as typifying a railway's house style, in which the locomotives of a particular line bore a close family resemblance to each other. (Colin Alexander)

What would become L&NER Class C4 is another locomotive type widely considered to be the most handsome. In 1903, Beyer Peacock built the first of an eventual total of twenty-seven Class 8B 4-4-2s for the Great Central Railway, designed by Robinson. They were given the nickname 'Jersey Lilies' for their good looks, after the Victorian star of the stage Lillie Langtry. It is difficult to see how her outline or proportions could be improved in any way. (ETH Zurich)

Beneath the shabby exterior, the outsized headlight and cowcatcher lies a classic British 4-4-0. This is one of hundreds of BESA (British Engineering Standards Association) locomotives exported to India by several British locomotive manufacturers. No. 3191 is a 4-4-0 of SP (standard passenger) type, and was photographed in her latter years in Pakistan. (Alon Siton collection)

In contrast to the many thousands of British-built locomotives that were exported, it was rare for foreign-built engines to run in this country. A notable exception was in 1903, when the Great Western Railway imported the first of a trio of Alfred De Glehn's compound 4-4-2s from France. No. 103 *President* is seen here at Paddington, having received a GWR tapered boiler in 1910. Overseas locomotive engineers were certainly capable of achieving a neat appearance on occasion! (Alon Siton collection)

The bespoke cut-down cab for the low tunnels under Sunderland does not detract from the appearance of 1904-built Kitson 0-6-2T No. 29, built for hauling coal on the Lambton Hetton & Joicey Railway. She is one of two preserved at the North Yorkshire Moors Railway, where she is seen passing Darnholm during a period of running in, on 30 July 2019. (Colin Alexander)

Compare Harry Wainwright's H Class 0-4-4T with his 0-6-0 No. 592 and it is clear that he had an eye for the aesthetic. In this idyllic scene, No. 263 is departing Horsted Keynes on the Bluebell Railway in the spring sunshine of March 2014. It is at the head of a rake of beautiful period stock. (Andrew Shapland)

Conveying an impression of power, this is a 1905-built BESA HPS Class 4-6-0, the big sister of No. 3191 (see p. 52). No. 1143 was built at Vulcan Foundry, Newton-le-Willows, and looks every inch the British thoroughbred, despite the external additions required by Indian practice. (Alon Siton collection)

Descended from Ivatt's Great Northern Atlantics, the first of Marsh's Class H1 4-4-2s for the London, Brighton & South Coast Railway appeared in 1905. The scrapping of the last of these fine-looking locomotives was a tragedy, now being put right by the building of new-build No. 32424 *Beachy Head* at Sheffield Park. No. 39, seen here, was named *La France* in 1913. (ETH Zurich)

As the Edwardian era progressed, goods locomotives increasingly tended to wear plain black livery, as well as growing in dimension. This is ex-GER, L&NER Class J17 0-6-0 No. 8217, built in 1905 and rebuilt in 1921. She is preserved and was photographed in the roundhouse at Barrow Hill on 20 August 2016. Her neat, modern appearance makes an interesting aesthetic comparison with SE&CR No. 592 seen earlier. (Colin Alexander)

One of the earliest exponents of the 2-6-2T wheel arrangement in Britain was George Jackson Churchward on the GWR. His Class 45xx tanks first appeared in 1906, a development of the smaller 44xx. Happily, many are preserved. No. 4566 resides at the Severn Valley Railway, where she is seen undergoing maintenance at Bridgnorth shed in the late 1980s. (John Alexander MBE)

Similar in many respects to Billinton's B4s on the LB&SCR, the SE&CR's Class E 4-4-0 was introduced in 1906 and rebuilt in 1918 into the form seen here, known as Class E1. This is an example of the archetypal early twentieth-century inside-cylindered 4-4-0 passenger engine, with raised running plate, Belpaire firebox and commodious cab. (ETH Zurich)

The culmination in the development of the North Eastern Railway's goods 0-6-0 was Wilson Worsdell's 1906 large-boilered Class P3. These sturdy and purposeful-looking engines became L&NER J27 and were very long-lived, lasting until the end of steam in the North East, in 1967. The North Eastern Locomotive Preservation Group saved BR No. 65894 from scrap, and she is seen here passing Darnholm on the North Yorkshire Moors Railway on 1 June 2018. (Colin Alexander)

The 4-6-0 wheel arrangement became the standard type for express passenger work in the years leading up to the First World War. The year 1906 saw McIntosh's Cardean Class appear on the Caledonian Railway, such as No. 903, seen here. They were considered by A. J. Lewer to be one of the most beautiful locomotives ever built, with the sweeping 'wings' supporting the smokebox. He also notes the visual 'triangle' formed by the chimney placed centrally over the leading bogie wheels, and the large driving wheel splashers, which graduate upwards from the subsidiary coupling rod splashers. (ETH Zurich)

Providing some contrast is SC3 Class 2-8-0 No. 29 of the Grand Canyon Railway at Williams, Arizona, in August 2013. A product of Alco in 1906, she is powerful and imposing, but the mass of exterior pipework and other fittings exemplifies the aesthetic difference between a typical British-outline locomotive and its American counterpart. (Colin Alexander)

The tank engine version of the 4-4-0 passenger engine was usually a 4-4-2T, with the extra rear carrying axle supporting the bunker, and they were invariably an attractive locomotive. The 1909-built London, Tilbury & Southend Railway No. 80 *Thundersley* is carrying extra decoration to mark the coronation of George V; it was, however, a bespoke design with no tender-loco equivalent. (ETH Zurich)

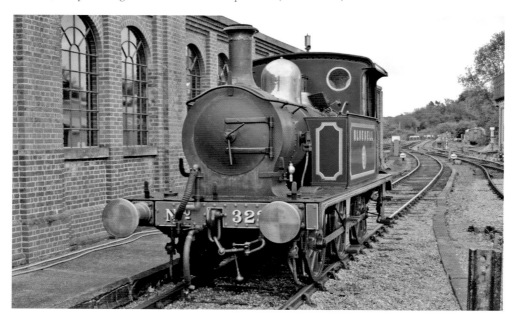

Another attractive Wainwright design for the SE&CR was his P Class 0-6-0T of 1909, which was loosely based on Stroudley's Terriers on the neighbouring LB&SCR, but with the trademark Wainwright flared cab roof. Remarkably, four of the eight locomotives that were built survive in preservation, including No. 323, seen here at Sheffield Park on the Bluebell Railway, whose preservation-era name and livery she carries. (Colin Alexander)

We are staying on the theme of diminutive tank engines, but this time it is an outside-cylindered saddle tank designed by Churchward for the GWR in 1910. His 1361 Class 0-6-0ST was designed to negotiate sharp radius curves, and No. 1363 is preserved at Didcot. (Ian J. Robinson)

In the same year, Churchward introduced a tank engine at the other end of the scale – his heavy freight 2-8-0T. Several examples of these imposing locomotives are preserved, including No. 4270 seen at Winchcombe on the Gloucestershire & Warwickshire Railway on 27 May 2019. (Peter Stott)

This period was clearly a busy time for Churchward as he modernised the GWR's motive power fleet. The year 1911 saw the introduction of his versatile and handsome 2-6-0, of which over 300 were built. Two are preserved including No. 5322 at Didcot, where she was photographed on 29 August 2018. (Steve Richards)

One of the most famous British locomotive types in history was Robinson Class 8K 2-8-0, introduced on the Great Central Railway in 1911. Their good looks are incidental, however, compared to the work they did. They became the locomotive of choice for the Railway Operating Division, later the War Department, and saw extensive service overseas in both world wars. This wonderful photo is from the collection of Sgt-Major Harold Isted Hopper RFC/RAF & RNAS, and shows ROD No. 1680 on active duty in France. She was also used in the Second World War. (Alon Siton collection)

The sylvan setting of Sunniside, at the north end of the Tanfield Railway in County Durham, sees delightful 0-4-0ST No. 2, built in 1911 by Hawthorn Leslie of Newcastle. Despite her humble role at Keighley Corporation Gas Works, she was still delivered with brass fittings and given a fetching lined green colour scheme. (Colin Alexander)

The 4-4-2 wheel arrangement usually led to naturally visually pleasing locomotives. Combining power and grace, 1911-built North British Railway Atlantic No. 902 *Highland Chief* was built by Robert Stephenson & Co. Notice how boiler diameters continued to increase, which in turn led to reduced-height boiler mountings in order to stay within loading gauge. (Alon Siton collection)

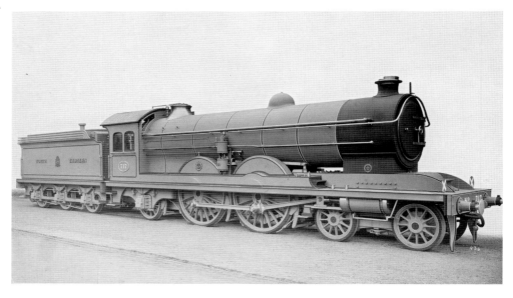

By way of comparison, the North Eastern Railway was also building Atlantics in 1911. Sir Vincent Raven, having replaced Worsdell, designed the beautiful Class Z 4-4-2 with its straight running plate, distinctive elongated splashers and round-topped firebox. No. 717 was built by the North British Locomotive Co., Glasgow. (ETH Zurich)

This is preserved North British Railway K Class (L&NER D34) 4-4-0 No. 256 *Glen Douglas* in the shed at Bo'ness on 16 August 2003. She now resides in the Riverside Museum in Glasgow along with other important and unique survivors from north of the border. The NBR was another Scottish company that adorned the smokeboxes of its locomotives with a star motif. Its bronze-green livery was distinctive and attractively lined. (David Ward)

ARN. JUNG, LOKOMOTIVFABRIK, JUNGENTHAL
BEI KIRCHEN/SIEG (RHEINL.)

Locomotive à marchandises, à 3/4 essieux accouplés avec tender séparé à 3 essieux.
à voie de 1435 mm ayant un poids en service de 102 tonnes et étant munie du réchauffeur système Caille-Potonié.

Compare the clean lines of any of the British locomotives in this volume with the raw functionality of this ungainly 2-6-0 built by Jung Lokomotivfabrik of Germany in 1913, for service in Romania. Her elevated boiler with multiple mountings and exposed motion, which was designed for ease of maintenance, seem to give her a cluttered and top-heavy appearance. (Alon Siton collection)

Back in Britain, meanwhile, by 1913 we are starting to see some seriously large locomotives, but again without aesthetic compromise. The L&NWR's Claughton four-cylinder 4-6-0 was designed for heavy express passenger work by Charles Bowen Cooke and combined power with beauty. The long-lost Claughton is another example of a new-build scheme in progress. This is No. 2401 *Lord Kitchener*. (ETH Zurich)

Another 4-6-0, but with smaller wheels and only two cylinders for mixed-traffic use, was the L&SWR H15 Class, designed by Robert Urie. They were introduced in 1914 and lasted until 1961, the design being developed into the more numerous S15. No. 331 shows off her modern lines in Southern Railway days, with high running plate and outside Walschaerts valve gear. (ETH Zurich)

Illustrating another example of the British aesthetic as applied to locomotives for export, as well as the versatility of domestic manufacturers, is this metre-gauge 2-8-0, built in 1914 by Robert Stephenson & Co. for the Leopoldina Railway in Brazil. No. 221 was later used by the Usina Santo Amaro, under whose ownership she heads a trainload of sugar cane towards Baixa Grande in 1985. (Alon Siton collection)

In 1914, Billinton built seven of these massive 4-6-4T engines for express passenger work on the LB&SCR. No. 2331 looks magnificent in the livery of the Southern Railway, the company that, in order to increase coal and water capacity, was to rebuild them all as slightly less impressive 4-6-0 tender locomotives. (Alon Siton collection)

Among the most handsome 2-8-0 types ever built was this bespoke design for the hilly Somerset & Dorset Joint Railway. A total of eleven were constructed – six at Derby and five at Stephenson's – from 1914 to 1925. Two are preserved including No. 88, seen here at Minehead on the West Somerset Railway on 2 September 2012. (Colin Alexander)

By 1918, the London & South Western Railway was in need of new express passenger power, so Robert Urie designed his Class N15 4-6-0, known as King Arthurs. They were developed by his Southern Railway successor Richard Maunsell, who continued production. One of the later versions, 1925-built No. 777 *Sir Lamiel*, is preserved, as seen on the excellent Great Central Railway at Loughborough on 4 March 2017. (Colin Alexander)

One of the most successful locomotive types on the original Great Central Railway (as opposed to its preserved incarnation) was the 1919 Improved Director Class 4-4-0, designed by Robinson. In L&NER days, as Class D11, construction continued. They could be seen far beyond former GCR territory at this time. No. 506 *Butler Henderson* is preserved and was seen at Barrow Hill on 1 July 2012. The continuous splashers and deep red frames form a harmonious composition. (Colin Alexander)

Another iconic locomotive type lost to scrap, introduced the same year as *Butler Henderson*, was the GWR's 47xx 2-8-0, designed by Churchward. Compared to the 28xx seen earlier, they had larger driving wheels for working express freight trains. They were versatile and saw use on heavy passenger trains too. No. 4705 is seen on shed beside a BR Class 9F 2-10-0. We will all be able to enjoy a 47xx in action again, thanks to another new-build project. (Bob Lovelock)

Kitson's of Leeds were responsible for the building of five of these enormous inside-cylindered 4-6-4T locomotives for the Furness Railway. It is arguable whether having the motion between the frames improves the aesthetics of a locomotive. The reader can decide by making comparisons with the Brighton 4-6-4T seen earlier, and the Lancashire & Yorkshire Railway variation on the following pages, both of which had outside cylinders. (Alon Siton collection)

The Great North of Scotland Railway relied almost entirely on locomotives of the 4-4-0 wheel arrangement, and very attractive they were too. As late as 1920, North British of Glasgow was building locomotives of such charmingly Victorian appearance as No. 54 here, with her beautiful curved splashers. (Alon Siton collection)

Britain's first 4-6-2 was Churchward's No. 111 *The Great Bear* on the GWR, but it was not a great success. The same can be said for Raven's Pacifics for the NER. Contemporary with the latter engines, Sir Nigel Gresley introduced his A1 Class on the GNR in 1922. They took advantage of their wheel arrangement with their deep, wide fireboxes and, when developed by the L&NER as the superheated Class A3, they were superb performers. No.4472 *Flying Scotsman* is seen here at Carnforth around 1983. (Colin Alexander)

No. 1472, later 4472, was the third member of the class and arguably became the most famous locomotive in the world. She became BR No. 60103, having achieved fame when she was the first locomotive in the world to reach an authenticated 100 mph in 1934. Sister locomotive No. 2750 *Papyrus* broke that record, hitting 108 mph, paving the way for Gresley's streamliners. (Colin Alexander)

In contrast to the glamour of Gresley's thoroughbred Pacific, but still displaying classic British lines, this work-weary 1922-built 4-6-0 was built by the North British Locomotive Company of Glasgow for service in India. (Alon Siton collection)

15-inch-gauge 2-8-2 *River Esk* was purpose-built in 1923 by Davey, Paxman & Co. for the Ravenglass & Eskdale Railway in Cumberland. She originally featured a separate set of driven wheels beneath her tender, but this was subsequently removed. Despite her size, she is an aesthetic masterpiece of British engineering, especially when set against the dramatic backdrop of the Eskdale fells. (Tim Hagan)

The grouping of 1923 affected the GWR far less than the constituents of the other three new railway companies. In terms of livery its locomotives remained more or less unchanged, retaining the traditional copper and brass fittings. Collett's 1923 development of Churchward's four-cylinder Star Class 4-6-0 was the iconic Castle Class, one of the most successful express passenger locomotives of all time. Preserved No. 5051 *Drysllwyn Castle* looks magnificent at Didcot in 2009. (Ian J. Robinson)

The following year saw the emergence from Swindon of Collett's Hall Class, evolved from Churchward's Saints. The Halls played a major role in the modernisation of the GWR fleet and could be said to be the progenitor of Stanier's Black Five 4-6-0s. No. 6960 *Raveningham Hall* was at Williton on the West Somerset Railway on 2 September 2012. (Colin Alexander)

Once again, the humble, well-proportioned 0-6-0T. This is the LM&SR Class 3F ('Jinty'), a locomotive I always loved, thanks to my Tri-ang OO-gauge model as a child. They were a development of a Midland Railway design and some were operated by the Somerset & Dorset Joint Railway, in whose livery is No. 7327, masquerading as S&DJR No. 23 inside the shed at Swanwick, Midland Railway Centre. (Colin Alexander)

Also dating from 1924 were Hughes' massive four-cylinder 4-6-4 tanks, ordered by the Lancashire & Yorkshire Railway but not delivered until LM&SR days. Mechanically, they were not a total success, but as a visual essay in steel they were incredibly impressive. No. 11114 is posed here for her official works portrait. Sister locomotive No. 11111 was apparently nicknamed 'Packet of Woodbines'. (Alon Siton collection)

In 1926, Maunsell introduced a new four-cylinder 4-6-0 intended to work heavy boat trains on the Southern Railway at speeds that would not hinder suburban electric trains around London. All were named after famous admirals and became known as the 'Lord Nelson' Class. No. 851 *Sir Francis Drake* exudes power in this portrait, and would look even more imposing with the later addition of smoke deflectors. (ETH Zurich)

Also on the Southern in 1926, a class of 2-6-4T engines entered service, but were rebuilt in 1928 following a number of serious derailments. The outcome of rebuilding was a series of twenty good-looking 2-6-0s of Class U, of which one, No. 31806, is preserved. She is seen at Kidderminster, Severn Valley Railway, on 14 October 2012. (Tony Hisgett)

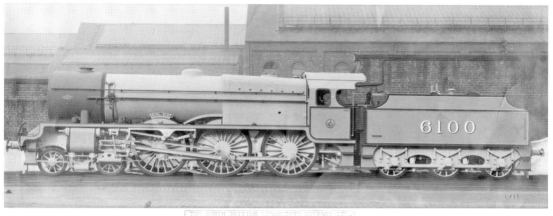

Making an interesting comparison with Southern No. 851 is LM&SR Fowler 4-6-0 6100 *Royal Scot* of 1927. She was said to be a three-cylinder derivation of Maunsell's big 4-6-0s, for which Fowler was supplied the drawings by the Southern Railway. *Royal Scot* and her sisters were the mainstay of West Coast express workings for several years. (Alon Siton collection)

The Scots were rebuilt with taper boilers by Fowler's successor, Stanier, but with no detrimental effect to their appearance. Now preserved as BR No. 46100, *Royal Scot* is seen passing Stow in the Scottish Borders on the recently reopened northern section of the legendary Waverley route, in August 2016. (Ian J Robinson)

Above and opposite page: The ultimate expression of GWR passenger power was Collett's King Class 4-6-0, which appeared in 1927. No. 6023 *King Edward II* may displease Swindon purists in the short-lived BR express blue livery. Unlike the other Big Four companies, the GWR continued the tradition of cast number plates on its locomotives, which went beautifully with the curved brass nameplates. These photos were taken at Toddington on the Gloucestershire & Warwickshire Railway in 2018. (Paul Jones)

On a slightly smaller scale, 1927 also saw the debut of Gresley's D49 Class 4-4-0 on the L&NER. They were designed for secondary passenger services and were among the last new locomotives of this aesthetically pleasing wheel arrangement. One is preserved, No. 246 *Morayshire*, and is seen here at Doncaster works in 2003. (Colin Alexander)

The pannier tank was synonymous with the Great Western Railway, and they were very useful good-looking engines. Introduced in 1929, the 57xx Class 0-6-0PT became one of the most numerous types ever to run in Britain. No. 7714 is one of several preserved and is seen in BR black livery at Bewdley, on the Severn Valley Railway, in August 2018. (Colin Alexander)

Also in 1929, the first of Collett's development of Churchward's 'Large Prairie' tanks appeared. GWR 2-6-2T No. 4160 was at Minehead, West Somerset Railway, in September 2012. In lined green livery with brass number plate and copper chimney cap, she is just about as glamorous as a BR tank locomotive could get. (Colin Alexander)

A contemporary of Collett's 'Large Prairies', this 2-6-2T was built in 1930 for the LM&SR to the design of Henry Fowler. No. 15530 is in the company of two much earlier generations of ex-Midland Railway tank engines of the 0-4-4T wheel arrangement. Although Fowler's 2-6-2Ts were not as successful as those on the GWR, I think they are equally attractive. (ETH Zurich)

Staying with the Prairie tank theme, Sir Nigel Gresley's locomotives were invariably of very pleasing proportions, and his V1 and V3 Class 2-6-2Ts, introduced in 1930, were no exception. No. 67656 is seen here at Newcastle Central station in 1963, and no amount of accumulated grime can hide her beauty. None survived into preservation. (Alan Leslie)

Another of Fowler's 1930 designs for the LM&SR was his Patriot, a lighter version of the Royal Scot Class. They were particularly pretty 4-6-0s, but sadly all were scrapped, including No. 45511 *Isle Of Man*, seen here at Crewe works on 10 June 1956. As this book goes to press, a new Patriot, No. 5551 *The Unknown Warrior* is in the advanced stages of being constructed. (Reproduced by kind permission of the RCTS Archive)

Britain's last, and by far most powerful, class of 4-4-0 was Maunsell's Class V for the Southern Railway. Introduced in 1930 and known as the Schools Class, they were three-cylinder express passenger locomotives designed specifically for the restricted route to Hastings. Three of these handsome machines are preserved, including No. 926 *Repton* on the North Yorkshire Moors Railway, where she is seen in all her glory at Grosmont in June 2018. (Colin Alexander)

Two years later, across the Irish Sea, saw the debut of a different Class V 4-4-0. The Great Northern Railway (Ireland)'s Vs were the most famous design of George T. Glover, who came from the North Eastern Railway. They were the first three-cylinder engines in Ireland, cutting twenty-two minutes off the schedule for Dublin to Belfast expresses. No. 85 Merlin is preserved in working order by the Railway Preservation Society of Ireland and is the last full-sized compound at work in the British Isles. (Richard Vogel)

Was there ever a neater tank locomotive design than Collett's 14xx 0-4-2T for the Great Western Railway? They were introduced in 1932, the natural successor to the Victorian Metro tanks. Four are preserved, including No. 1450, seen here at Bewdley on the Severn Valley Railway on 17 August 2018. (Colin Alexander)

By the mid-1930s, increased traffic on the West Coast Main Line meant that the new chief mechanical engineer of the London Midland & Scottish Railway, William Stanier, had to design a powerful new 4-6-2 locomotive. The twelve members of the Princess Royal Class were of (in British terms) unprecedented dimensions. Two are preserved, one of which is No. 46203 *Princess Margaret Rose,* displayed at Crewe on 10 September 2005. (Trevor Casey)

Sister engine, and sister in real life, No. 6201 *Princess Elizabeth* is also preserved and, appropriately, her nameplate is surmounted by a crown. (Colin Alexander)

Gresley's P2 2-8-2s for the L&NER were surely among the most impressive locomotives ever to run in Britain. They were introduced in 1934 and designed for the Edinburgh to Aberdeen route. No. 2002 *Earl Marischal* was one of the first two, featuring elegant curved smoke deflectors incorporated into the boiler cladding. The four later examples were built with streamlined fronts similar to the A4s (q.v.), and the first pair were subsequently rebuilt along the same lines. All were rebuilt by Thompson in the 1940s as ungainly Pacifics, but schemes are underway to recreate two of the class as twenty-first-century new-builds. (Alon Siton collection)

Stanier was a busy man in the 1930s, as he set about standardising and modernising the locomotive fleet of the LM&SR. In 1934 the first of his ubiquitous, but very handsome, Black Five 4-6-0s appeared. They would eventually number 842 in total and many are preserved. No. 5428, named *Eric Treacy* in preservation, after the famous railway photographer and bishop, is seen here passing Fen Bog on the North Yorkshire Moors Railway. She was one of a batch built by Armstrong Whitworth in Newcastle. (Colin Alexander)

Stanier's Black Five was very much the archetypal mixed-traffic locomotive, whereas his contemporary Jubilee Class 4-6-0, with its larger driving wheels and three cylinders, was for express passenger work. Easily identifiable by their raised splashers and evocative names, the Jubilees were slightly more glamorous than the Fives. No. 45690 *Leander* was photographed at Carlisle Citadel on 5 June 2018. (Colin Alexander)

Looking very much the cousin of Stanier's 4-6-0 classes, his 8F 2-8-0s for heavy freight were among the most successful locomotives ever built. Introduced in 1935, hundreds would be built for the War Department, including No. 8233, seen at Bridgnorth on the Severn Valley Railway in the late 1970s. She was one of many 8Fs to serve overseas during the Second World War, seeing use in Iran and Egypt before being repatriated. (Alon Siton collection)

The year 1935 also saw the appearance of the first of Gresley's iconic A4 Class. They were a streamlined development of his A3, resulting in one of the most recognisable locomotive types in history. Of course, No. 4468 *Mallard* has gone down in history with her 1938 world speed record for steam traction of 126 mph, and she is rightly preserved in the National Railway Museum. Five of her sisters also survive, including No. 4464 *Bittern*, captured here in garter blue livery with red wheels at Grosmont on the North Yorkshire Moors Railway in May 2014. (Helen Cessford)

Possibly even more striking than *Bittern*'s blue livery, the first four A4s were turned out in two-tone silver-grey to match the colour scheme of the Silver Jubilee coaching stock, but even the relatively drab green livery applied by BR after nationalisation could not diminish the beauty of Gresley's streamliners. Note also how the valances over the wheels have been removed to assist maintenance – a wartime measure. No. 60009 *Union of South Africa* is being turned at Heaton depot, Newcastle, on 25 October 2014. (Ian Beattie)

Where other railways relied upon two-cylinder 4-6-0s for mixed-traffic use, in 1936 Gresley introduced his three-cylinder V2 Class 2-6-2, the first of which was No. 4771 *Green Arrow*. A total of 184 were built and they have been called 'the engines that won the war', for their sterling wartime work hauling prodigious loads in difficult conditions. In my opinion they were simply the most handsome, balanced, purposeful-looking locomotives of all time. (Colin Alexander)

The outside-framed GWR Cities were anachronistic enough at the dawn of the twentieth century, so it is even more remarkable that another visually similar class of 4-4-0s appeared in that company's livery the year after Gresley's A4s made their debut. In truth, the 'Dukedogs', as they became known, utilised the frames of withdrawn Bulldogs with the boilers from Dukes. No. 9017 *Earl of Berkeley* is preserved on the Bluebell Railway, where she looks superb coupled to a milk tanker in February 2009. (John Ellender)

Yet another beautiful Gresley design for the L&NER was his 1937 Class K4 2-6-0, designed specifically to handle the gradients of the West Highland line to Mallaig. BR No. 61994 *The Great Marquess* survives in preservation and was in steam at Pickering, on the North Yorkshire Moors Railway, on 26 August 2015. (Colin Alexander)

Following his Princess Royals, Stanier developed his Pacific design further, producing an even more powerful 4-6-2 in 1937. Eyeing the blaze of publicity that had accompanied the launch of Gresley's A4s, the first batch of the new Princess Coronations were also encased in streamlining. I find the casing on Stanier's Pacifics rather vulgar and bulbous in comparison to Gresley's A4s. They were very impressive locomotives, however, and first of the class, No. 6220 *Coronation*, seen here in original condition, reached the speed of 114 mph. (Alon Siton collection)

There are few sights finer than a magnificent steam locomotive passing through the wild British landscape. Stanier removed the streamlining from his Pacifics, and more were built along more conventional lines. They were truly handsome machines too. This is No. 6233 *Duchess of Sutherland* at Bessygill, between Penrith and Shap, on the West Coast Main Line in 2009. (Craig Oliphant)

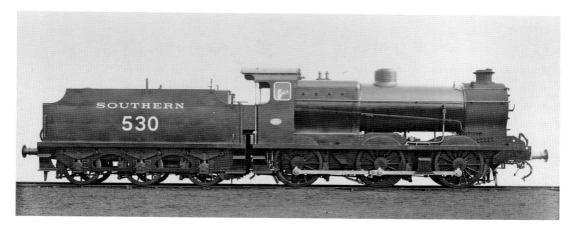

From the glamour of streamlined Pacifics to the mundane goods 0-6-0. One of the last types of this classic wheel arrangement was Maunsell's Q Class 0-6-0 of 1938. A no-nonsense, neat, functional locomotive, it could be said to be the descendant of the Midland 3F or the GER Y14, with modern features. No. 530 is seen here in an official portrait, and sister No. 541 is preserved on the Bluebell Railway. (ETH Zurich)

Collett's Great Western Railway Manor Class of 1938 was the lightweight version of his 4-6-0. They were of very pleasing proportions and, as was customary at Swindon, they were adorned with copper chimney caps and brass fittings. No. 7802 *Bradley Manor* is one of several preserved, and is seen here raising steam at Bewdley on the Severn Valley Railway on 20 May 2018. (Colin Alexander)

Across the Irish Sea, in 1939, the Inchicore Works of the Great Southern Railway turned out three 4-6-0s, the largest and most powerful locomotives ever built in Ireland, and they were just as handsome as any British 4-6-0. While every other locomotive on the GSR wore plain grey livery, this trio were given a special lined green scheme. No. 800 *Maedb/Maeve* is preserved in the Ulster Folk and Transport Museum in Cultra, as seen here. (Morgan Young)

Oliver Bulleid, who replaced Maunsell as the Southern Railway's locomotive engineer, is best known for his controversial 4-6-2 classes. Introduced in 1945, his 'light Pacifics', known as West Country and Battle of Britain Classes featured the same 'air-smoothed' casing and Boxpok wheels as their larger, Merchant Navy predecessors. They may not be to everyone's liking but they were certainly distinctive and very imposing. Preserved No. 34092 *City of Wells* is seen in action at Grosmont on the North Yorkshire Moors Railway in 2019. (Colin Alexander)

The scrolled nameplates and coats of arms attached to each member of the West Country Class was a nice aesthetic touch, as seen at Bury, East Lancashire Railway in 2018. (Colin Alexander)

Many of Bulleid's 'light Pacifics' were rebuilt in more conventional form by BR, a fate that befell all of his Merchant Navy Class. This entailed the removal of their air-smoothed casing and unconventional valve gear. The result was a very handsome and modern-looking 4-6-2. Preserved Merchant Navy No. 35005 *Canadian Pacific* gets away from Toddington on the Gloucestershire & Warwickshire Railway on 10 September 2005. (Paul Jones)

Edward Thompson replaced Gresley as chief mechanical engineer of the L&NER, and his most successful design was undoubtedly the Class B1 4-6-0, of which 410 examples were built from 1942. They were very much the equivalent of the GWR Hall and LM&SR Black Five, and, unlike some of Thompson's locomotives, they were quite attractive too. This is one of two preserved, No. 61264, between turns at Heaton depot, Newcastle, on 28 March 2014. (Ian Beattie)

The final design in the long line of GWR 4-6-0s was Hawksworth's County Class of 1945. Visual differences from their predecessors include the continuous splasher, straight nameplate and double chimney, but the aesthetic lineage can be traced back to Churchward's masterpieces. No. 1009 *County of Carmarthen* was photographed at Shrewsbury shed, around 1960. None survived the cull of the early 1960s, but a new-build replica is under construction. (Hancock collection)

The Northern Counties Committee operated railways in Northern Ireland, and was administered by the LM&SR. It is therefore unsurprising that many of its locomotives echoed the designs of the parent company. Preserved 2-6-4T No. 4 was a 1946 product of Derby works and bears many similarities with LM&SR 2-6-2 and 2-6-4 tank locomotives. (Morgan Young)

The family resemblance is clear to see between the Irish 2-6-4T and Ivatt's 1946 2MT 2-6-2T No. 41241, seen at a snowy Haworth on the Keighley & Worth Valley Railway, 10 February 2012. This was a truly modern design, relatively easy to maintain and a precursor of the BR Standards. (Duncan Harris)

The tender locomotive version of Ivatt's 2-6-2T was also introduced in 1946, and the two types shared many parts in common. Preserved Class 2MT 2-6-0 No. 46521 was photographed at Loughborough on the Great Central Railway in 2017. Some may argue that these post-war engines lacked some of the elegance of their Victorian equivalents, but they are far from ugly. (Colin Alexander)

Gresley's successor, Thompson, designed some Pacifics of strange proportions but this was put right by Arthur Peppercorn in 1947 with his version of the A2 Class 4-6-2. Sole survivor, No. 60532 *Blue Peter* is seen inside the magnificent Barrow Hill roundhouse on 1 July 2012. (Colin Alexander)

Introduced in 1949, the year after nationalisation, but having been ordered by the L&NER, the Class K1 2-6-0 was a Peppercorn development of a Thompson prototype. Of very neat appearance, No. 62005 is the only survivor of a class of seventy and is preserved by the North Eastern Locomotive Preservation Group. She was seen at Grosmont on the North Yorkshire Moors Railway on 8 April 2004. More recently, she has been one of the mainstays of the Jacobite trains on the West Highland line. (Colin Alexander)

As late as 1949, the British small industrial saddle tank was little changed, aesthetically, from its nineteenth-century ancestor. This is Peckett 0-4-0ST No. 2111 *Lytham St Annes*, built for use at Blackpool Gasworks, looking resplendent in blue livery with polished brass and copper. It is in service at the Midland Railway Centre, Butterley, Derbyshire, in 2017. (Colin Alexander)

The British 2-6-4 tank locomotive was usually of very handsome proportions, perhaps never more so than in its ultimate form, Robert Riddles' BR Standard 4MT, introduced in 1951. The gently curved profile of the side tanks is a distinctive feature. Several of these useful and versatile engines are preserved, including No. 80136, seen here passing Darnholm on the North Yorkshire Moors Railway in June 2018. (Colin Alexander)

Of the 999 BR Standard locomotives constructed, the majority were designated for mixed traffic use. The exceptions were the 9F (see p. 95) and the solitary 8P 4-6-2 for express passenger use, No. 71000 *Duke of Gloucester*. She was also the only three-cylinder Standard and, although perhaps lacking some of the finesse and grace of earlier British Pacifics, she is nonetheless a magnificent sight and a remarkable preservation survivor. (Paul Jones)

The culmination of steam locomotive development in Britain was the BR Standard Class 9F 2-10-0, comprising 251 engines. Even this most modern of designs, built between 1954 and 1960, displays clean lines and a neatness of appearance; however, some purists might criticise the high running plate, designed for easy access to the motion. The very last of all, No. 92220 *Evening Star* was embellished with copper chimney cap and lined green livery, an appropriate conclusion to a 130-year timeline of engineering elegance. Sister loco No. 92214 is seen at Loughborough, Great Central Railway, wearing a non-authentic version of BR green livery. (Colin Alexander)

The final chapter in the story of the L&NER Pacifics was Peppercorn's Class A1, which embodied every available modern refinement when they were introduced in the early days of British Railways. Sadly, all were scrapped, but thanks to the A1 Steam Locomotive Trust, in an amazing story of vision and determination, a completely new 4-6-2 locomotive in the shape of No. 60163 *Tornado* emerged from the original drawings, paving the way for many more new-build projects, recreating some of Britain's long-lost examples of engineering elegance. Here she is, drawing the crowds at Pickering on the North Yorkshire Moors Railway in 2013. (Mark Cessford)

Also available from Amberley Publishing

NORTH BRITISH
LOCOMOTIVE COMPANY
COLIN ALEXANDER | ALON SITON

n all good bookshops or to order direct
Please call **01453-847-800**
ww.amberley-books.com